Ardelean Gheorghe Cornel (BIGAGC)

MEDITATIONS
VOL.8

NARCOSIA Publishing -2008

Reading and applying these, quotes, ideas
1) You save time, self-training and accumulatea lot of useful information immediately.
2) You manage to achieve your personal goals much faster, more efficiently.
3) You manage to prevent many unpleasant surprises, mistakes, failures, problems, illnesses, etc.
4) You manage to become more optimistic, more positive, more creative, more adaptable, more flexible, more efficient, more confident in yourself, more constructive, etc.
ABOUT ME
Rachel Mitchell AutorProducer TV/Film/ Documentaries – Director of Programming & Investor BUILTinAMERICA.tv
I appreciate every thing you wrote Ardelean Gheorghe Cornel (BIGAGC)you are a wealth of wisdom

Ardelean Gheorghe Cornel (BIGAGC)

MEDITATIONS
VOL. 8

NARCOSIA Publishing
ARAD COUNTY, MACEA
2008

CIP description of the Romanian National Library

Ardelean Gheorghe Cornel (BIGAGC)

ISBN 978-973-88998-0-3
ISBN 978-973-88998-7-2

Urge to read, analyze and apply these meditations

By reading and analyzing the meditations of (BIGAGC) by applying one or more thoughts we will find solutions that will help us:

I. Discover:
1. qualities;
2. defects;
3. capabilities;
4. skills;
5. some opportunities to succeed in life;
6. finding a partner for life;
7. keeping our marriage;
8. discovering our feelings;
9. discovering our mistakes;
10. etc..

II. To prevent some:
1. mistakes;
2. accidents;
3. divorces;
4. trouble;
5. bankruptcies;
6. failures;
7. conflicts;
8. etc..

III. Become:
1. more efficient;
2. happier;
3. more loved;
4. more honorable;
5. appreciated;
6. more respected;
7. more loved;
8. more organized;

9. more optimistic;
10. more plan;
11. most active;
12. best;
13. fairer;
14. more humane;
15. more unselfish;
16. popular;
17. more famous;
18. etc..

IV. Come out of:
1. the state of lost hope;
2. the state of pessimism;
3. the state of despair;
4. the state of passivity;
5. the state of inactivity
6. etc..

V. Participate at:

1. social life;
2. political life;
3. the activity of non-profit organization
4. etc..

VI. Find more opportunities to meet favorable or more favorable conditions.

VII. To let us change our lives more in better, to make it more beautiful.

VIII. To expand our chances to find the right partner for life.

IX. To let us realize and to

maintain a happy marriage.

X. To let us raise and educate our children better, to take more care of them.

I am writing these meditations and adding these books, other publications and on the Internet, etc.. because we need them every day and it is necessary to apply them so that we each achieve what we want: a more beautiful life, a more prosperous and happy one. These meditations reflect a tiny part of reality, of what would be good to be present in real life and in human relations.

I expect good news from you, good deeds that you have done influenced by the fact that you have read and applied one or more ideas to make your life more beautiful, more prosperous, more happy and to be positive lively models for others.

Each of us can become a positive new model for those around us thus participating in the creation of a better human society, of a more prosperous one, and a happier one.

I would be very happy and excited if one or more ideas that you have read, help you in one way or another or make you happier, more prosperous, etc..

I wish you all health, happiness and the achieving of all things that you want.

I expect your news, ideas, opinions, troubles and joys, etc..

Sincerely, love and with much joy,
I invite you to visit my site http://www.bigagc.com and to write to me at: aradforex@gmail.com

"Ardelean Gheorghe Cornel"
(BIGAGC)

VOLUME 8

1)	Many people in life have favorable circumstances but do not know how to use them in their favor.

2)	People who live in favorable circumstances also use them in life to achieve more bigger or smaller successes.

3)	It is necessary that each of us learns to see favorable circumstances and to use them in our favor.

4)	In life, we have much more favorable circumstances if we have knowledge in many different areas. Because this is necessary for our own good to accumulate as long as we live as much knowledge in many areas as we can.

5)	He who is realistic needs to meet the required one or more of his needs or of others.

6) A personal project can bring us a lot of joy, satisfaction, fulfillment if we achieve it.

7) Always in the creation and establishment of personal projects we must take into account our knowledge, qualities, abilities and our skills.

8) If we establish personal projects for whose achievement we do not have the necessary knowledge, skills, qualities and abilities, we are very likely not to achieve them.

9) Creative people are always young spirituals.

10) People who are always concerned about the future also have creative qualities.

11) Creative people have a futurological thought on a long term.

12) Creative people have a great capacity to create projects.

13)	People can develop their creative potential for as long as they live.

14)	Man for as long as he lives can continuously increase his capacity to create, set and achieve personal projects.

15)	Continuous learning leads those who practice it to achieve many bigger or smaller successes.

16)	People who have no personal projects live life at chance.

17)	To develop as a person it is necessary to make a personal goal to develop and do not want to leave to chance our performance.

18)	In life we evolve very much as if we set for as long as we live a personal goal and objective to develop and move continuously, organized, planned and effective ways to achieve it.

19)	Those who have a personal goal for performance have very high chances to have more and greater successes for as long as they live, more joy, more satisfaction and happiness.

20)	In everyday life we find a lot of live models, who have as a personal goal to evolve, which have achieved many bigger or smaller successes, joy and much happiness and satisfaction from whom we can take many effective positive behaviors to help us greatly in achieving our objective to evolve and to avoid many mistakes.

21)	It is always needed to develop capacities, skills, qualities and attitudes, but we need the development of our personality, it is necessary to have this as a personal objective.

22)	Constructive thinking was, is and will be irreplaceable in the development of our personality.

23)	In life it is necessary and required to

be able to have that personal goal as we continue the development of constructive thinking.

24)	When we think constructively not destructively, we think this helps us prevent many mistakes, failures, accidents, divorces, misfortunes, conflicts, which are bad, harmful to us or others.

25)	All those who have achieved in life more bigger or smaller successes mostly had a constructive thinking.

26)	Those who have had a negative thinking in certain situations had many troubles, failures, conflicts in the family, some came to divorce, and they have achieved little success too.

27)	In the development of our personality an important role may be played by the help in multiple forms, of family, friends, colleagues from school, work, neighbors, all of which are related.

28)   In life we can increase the chances of bigger or smaller successes through the implementation of effective relationships as many and as continuous as possible.

29)   Constructive human relations, effective, harmonious ones help us greatly to achieve a beautiful life.

30)   The longer we are able to achieve more constructive human relationships, effective, harmonious ones, of mutual confidence, the more we will succeed more, the more certain we are to have a harmonious happy life, with more satisfactions, joy, successes and much happiness.

31)   Unfortunately in the world there are still far fewer constructive relations, effective, harmonious, mutual trust ones, compared to how many there could be.

32)   I have as a personal priority to achieve an increasing number of

constructive, effective, harmonious relations, with mutual trust with as many people as possible from all countries to cooperate effectively and support each other in achieving the personal objectives of each of us. Together we accomplish a lot of great deeds. I would be happy for people who read my writings and agree and apply one or more ideas to build as more and more efficient co operations as they can for each of us and for mankind. The possibilities and potential co operations are endless with me because I have projects in areas which may involve a large number of people. Waiting with confidence and very high expectations for your cooperation with concrete proposals in areas of activity and actions that we want to achieve and any idea, opinion, etc...

33) Constructive, efficient and

especially long term co operations, can lead to great achievements and we can get the most satisfaction, joy and happiness as we can.

34) Positive effective models, very useful to us, we find it necessary to look how they live: 1) studying as many biographies of people who have had great successes and achievements, 2) interviews and all that is written about people with success stories in the media and on the Internet; 3) direct discussion with people when we have successful opportunities, and continually seek to have the opportunity to discuss with people of success; 4) to work together with people of success; 5) through discussions with people who have known or worked with people of success; 6) with family members of successful people.

35) Persons with success, models of

their effective actions give us a positive incentive to achieve our objectives and personal milestones. For this reason, and that we can take positive and effective behavior from them, it is necessary to take more of their positive activities to effectively increase our efficiency and more our actions and achieve our personal goals.

36)   We can form courage and grow it by more positive, effective and planned behaviors. Among these are the continued developments of our knowledge in as many areas that can influence directly or indirectly our personal goals as possible. Usually, we are afraid to face the unknown. The longer we accumulate more knowledge we need in areas in which we act, the more we become more courageous, more confident in ourselves, with more success. Therefore, it is

necessary, useful and mandatory to develop what we need because it has multiple positive effects on us, besides the fact that we continuously increase our courage that we really need to achieve our personal goals.

37) As we have more knowledge necessary to achieve our personal goals the more courage we have.

38) We can continuously develop courage also through the experience we accumulate in one or more areas.

39) As we have more experience in a field of activity, we have more courage in actions and behaviors, projects we have in areas that we want to achieve them in.

40) I write to be useful and practical. He who writes every day to as many people as possible, helps them in one way or another, but as much as possible to help them achieve personal goals, brave

performances, with strong will, with perseverance, to get as much satisfaction, joy and happiness as they can, to develop a harmonious personality, to be part of as much love for as long as they live, a happy family with happy children, to be hardworking, wise, to have harmony in the family, to have as many relations of friendship and cooperation as they can, to be what makes them better for their family, children and others.

41)   A famous name creates riches but the riches are not the reputation if we lose it.

42)   A man's character can create many riches, but riches can not give back the character if it is lost.

43)   Negative, exaggerated pride can do so much harm in many situations.

44)   Wisdom helps us truly live, not to be taken by the waves of life at random.

45)   The lack of urgency in achieving personal goals in many cases leads us to many failures and to the lack of personal goals. It is good that we persevere to see this and to take the necessary steps to become perseverant in achieving all the objectives of our personal live.

46)   To succeed in life we must have respect for objectives and if not we will not succeed. Before it is necessary to know, understand and respect them when we need to. Those who respect them have many joys, satisfaction, success and much happiness in life. Is it worth the effort to know and to apply them.

47)   Although the rules of success in life are very simple, they are not known, unfortunately, by many people. It is of course understood that those who do not know the vast majority of them will not have many successes.

48)   People who have developed one or more successes have not stepped back before any effort required. Instead, they were not thinking and not scared to make great efforts that needed to be made in order to succeed.

49)   The size of our life is made up of several parts of what it is necessary to know very well in order to achieve each of them. It is not easy but not impossible. First we must know very clearly, concretely that we want to achieve each of them, when, how, we want to achieve them, etc... Among them we mention privacy that includes our family life, human relations with friends, our intimate life, our feelings and our thoughts, our intimate writings, journals, autobiographies, blogs, web pages etc. To succeed in this life it is necessary to respect, know the rules of success in this

private life. Then there is employment, which includes ideas, thoughts, actions, objectives and professional projects. And here in employment we can succeed only if we respect the rules needed to succeed in our careers. Good behavior is ideal when we can do that to support our private life as much as possible, employment contributes as much as possible to achieve a harmonious private life, with successful private joys, a lot of satisfactions and happiness. If we propose to realize these needs we will establish that we are able to achieve personal objectives and performance, great successes, and we will have joys, happiness and satisfactions in life, both in our private and professional one. Unfortunately, there are still few people who do what they should not do to have failures in both private and professional lives, or in one of them. The most happy and satisfying are called those who made the necessary efforts and who have managed to achieve harmonious, happy privacy, with joys and satisfactions and who have achieved personal goals and projects in employment. From them we can learn many effective models of action, positive behaviors, which will help us achieve our privacy and professionalism.

50)   Routine and daily habits should not be a brake for us, an impassable barrier in the form of our other more efficient, more orderly, faster, etc. behaviors.

51)   Those who fail to escape the routine of everyday habits have inefficient behavior, are messy, slow, chaotic, etc. and they will have many failures and few and small achievements in life.

52)   People who have a great capacity to take the needs of achieving personal goals, learn and take the behavior more efficient,

more orderly, faster, etc.; they will make life a lot more or less successful, will have many joys, much satisfaction and happiness and will do what they want in life.

53)   For those who have succeeded in life, who had one or more major successes, the effort they have made to pursue them without problems, to be consumed without having to make big efforts, they made such efforts on their own initiative, without them, someone would do them with great pleasure, without any stress, but it is considered that to succeed it is necessary to make those efforts, those actions. Although efforts, actions were very high, with huge consumption of mental and physical energy, more or less risks they felt of course, normal in order to achieve success, and what they proposed, and this is not to

look at the facts not stressed, but on the contrary it has created a state of normality and even additional motivation and desire to do what they have proposed. These ones in contrast with others that the risky, unpredictable, great efforts chased, tried to solve, or attempted to carry out the enormous stress and had much inefficient behavior, but they always made them smarter, more effective, more operational, more powerful, and more confident in their forces, in their success, in their future, etc...

54)   We should not be a slave to routine again, we must get rid of it and act differently, more effective, more operational, more tactful, more with courage from case to case depending on the situation.

55)   Those who are slaves to routine life and have many smaller or very big

failures, usually small achievements and successes, personal and professional unfulfillments, they are in fact slaves of their own inefficient, clumsy behaviors which affect their efficiency, their quality of the future etc..

56)   Routine is very necessary and useful in behavior, etc. in actions for a certain period of time. After a certain period of time, at a certain time it is necessary to get rid of a certain routine, a certain behavior, a way of thinking, a certain kind of action, etc... and replace it with another behavior more efficiently, more operational, more tactful, more thoughtful, etc... in order to progress in achieving what we proposed, our personal objectives. When we need to get rid, to escape a certain routine it is necessary to get rid of it immediately, without doubts, delay, fears, etc. and to act in the new action, new behavior more

effectively, without any delay. People who have the ability to leave a certain routine immediately when they need to, progress much faster in life, carry out much faster and more efficient personal goals, perform in live many more bigger or smaller successes than those who do not get rid of a particular or specific routine when necessary. Routine, when we get rid of it when necessary is a big negative factor of progress, it creates many failures, misfortunes, difficulties in achieving personal goals in life, it creates misunderstandings in families and may even lead to divorce, misunderstandings and even conflicts between large generations etc.. The routine of a normal fact, when we can not get rid of it, and it is necessary to get rid of it, it may actually become a very harmful fact for our new family, for the people around, for society, for younger generations and for the future, it may sometimes have many negative effects, very large and very diverse ones. For these reasons it is necessary to continuously develop our ability to get rid of routine when needed immediately.

57)   Each of us has had one or more bigger or smaller failures. It's good not to have any failures or as few failures as possible. Some or more failures could harm us very much. Those who were careful did not achieve failure or failures and have made smaller, fewer ones. Prevision helps us prevent many failures. The more experienced in previsioning we are, the greater ability we have to provide, as we have more knowledge necessary to achieve previsions etc... the more we can make accurate previsions, prevent many mistakes, failures, trouble, accidents, conflicts, arguments, unsuccessful actions,

etc. In our personal and professional life, it is necessary to continuously develop and to have that personal goal to develop to a maximum capacity the prevision in private life, the ability to use previsions. We can continuously increase the capacity of our prevision very much, as we live if we have personal objectives, as we expand our ability to prevision and whether we act to continuously and effectively achieve this objective.

Those who aimed at personal living as to develop the capacity of prevision continuously and concretely act with dedication to achieve their capacity to make a prevision which will help them achieve one or more very big successes, they will succeed to prevent many failures, troubles, etc., they will be able to achieve much in life, to have many happy, satisfying moments and so much happiness. The more we have a capacity of more than prevision, a more accurate, more efficient one, the more valuable we are for having this treasure. This treasure we can continuously increase greatly. The capacity of prevision generally contains more capacities of prevision in some actions, behaviors in the achievement of personal objectives, private, professional, specific ones, etc. It is necessary to develop those capabilities specific to prediction that we need. Knowledge, experience, qualifications, skills, etc., in a specific prevision capacity can be used to a greater or lesser degree in other capacities specific to prevision. The capacities of prevision are very necessary and very useful to us but unfortunately very few people have personal goals in life to continuously develop the specific performance of prevision. Due to the special importance of the capacity of prevision it is necessary and required to create and develop the science of the development of the capacity of prevision, because having this science we would have it by applying enormous positive effects on countless people that should develop and apply it indirectly on other people.

The state would accelerate progress in many fields, would accelerate the reduction of illiteracy, poverty, illness, divorces out of arguments and conflict, accidents, what harms humans, animals, the environment, etc... It would lead to solving many personal and state targets, it would create enormously many joys, much satisfaction and happiness. It would lead to the situation that most people no longer live at the whim of chance, with no personal, professional security, etc... but on the contrary they would lead to more people having them as an objective and as they continue to live, they would develop the personal capacities necessary for their prevision and apply them every day, both in the establishment of private personal or professional life, it would be something concrete that will help them achieve more harmonious lives to achieve what they want and need for their families.

There is the capacity of prevision in specific persons, specific societies, specific legal entities, nonprofit organizations, companies, banks, groups, collectivities, international and intergovernmental organizations. Both individuals and legal entities, must not live from hand to mouth, must act firmly, must study and evaluate the effects of positive and negative actions, decisions, etc. their objectives are also necessary to be: 1) to aim at continuing to develop their capacities of specific prediction that they need, 2) to apply, continuous use in any action, situation-specific prediction capabilities necessary and useful efforts, energy consumption and costs for the development and capacity of specific prevision that they need.

58) Failures can happen in each of our actions or less often. Our failures can be created by factors and actions sometimes difficult to identify and prevent. However there are actions where we can know all the factors that can create failures. Knowing the factors that create failures in actions, we can take the necessary measures to prevent them by reaching in some cases to zero failures, as they have succeeded in situations in a long time, in many states, especially people in the most developed countries of the world. How to

develop more this science with the more than we can know more of the factors that could cause failures in certain situations to certain actions. Scientific knowledge can contribute greatly to preventing many failures in many actions.

At present people do not use scientific knowledge, the human experience gained in books, studies, on the Internet, although they have committed enormously many failures, mistakes, although they could prevent many huge mistakes, failures if they would use efficient, organized, timely human experience and knowledge from books, the Internet when they would need it. Countries should take immediate measures and be more interested in people and use them when they need knowledge and human experience that can reach and can be used. Human knowledge is growing and increases daily awfully much, and human experience which can create the situation so that we can prevent every day more even more mistakes and failures with positive effects on our high society, to accelerate progress in many areas.

59)   Where we have failures we should never discourage and lose our wits, our balance inside, our optimism, morale or to start to grieve. If we do this, it would solve absolutely no problem, but on the contrary, it would stress us illogically, abnormally without any positive effects. Those who have achieved many successes knew how to cope with failure, learning from failures, to reduce the negative effects of failures.

Many failures rather than strengthening us, they weaken us, they should give us power instead of immobilizing us and mobilize us instead of making them harder to give motivation, instead of multiple negative effects they should have multiple positive effects. However, I disagree and do not consider as logical, positive or constructive the popular saying: „Man learns from mistakes". Man, on the contrary should learn only from his successes and from those who have achieved successes and gained, by imitating those positive behaviors, which have effectively contributed to success. In addition man can learn enormously not to have failures, or make mistakes from the knowledge and positive experience of mankind stored in books, media, on the Internet and the experience of people who have huge experience and knowledge. The more we can prevent more failures, mistakes, the more we can prevent more and more different negative effects.

60)   It would be necessary and useful the development of a science to prevent human errors because it would prevent a large number of human errors and failures if people study and apply it as much and in as many actions as they can. This knowledge could and should be studied in colleges and universities and other educational forms. In every area of activity for each action type, it could identify factors that create human mistakes and failures and then it could identify solutions and measures to be taken to prevent mistakes and failures.

61)   Efforts and expenses that will be done by creating, developing, learning and applying the science to prevent human errors will not be much lower than the positive effects of their prevention of a very large number of mistakes and failures and their multiple, diverse and very large

negative effects. Financial investment, energy, time, etc.. in these activities related to the prevention of human errors and failures would be very effective and necessary and useful for both countries and for people in particular. Each of us in a greater or lesser way can participate in the creation, development and application of the science to prevent human errors.

62)   Ideas come fast and we forget them even faster. Ideas come out continuously, without us making any effort. Ideas that we seek, that we want to find we sometimes find them easily, other times very difficult and sometimes we can not find anything without looking better.

63)   Our ability to create ideas is a mine which can increase the value and on a continuous basis, without great efforts.

64)   Our ability to create ideas can continuously increase for as long as we

live, thus increasing its value on a continuous basis. Our ability to create ideas affects us enormously in our achievement and maintenance of our happiness every day in every situation.

65) One of the objectives of each personal man is necessary and should be the continuous development as much as the ability to create useful, efficient, positive, humane ideas, which can contribute to the achievement of our personal happiness and maintain it.

66) As we grow with a grater ability to create positive, effective ideas, necessary to us, the more and more surely we can achieve personal goals and happiness and we can maintain them.

67) The ability to produce positive effective ideas, necessary to us is enormously useful and effective as it helps establish, develop, maintain other

capacities as well which we can exemplify: 1) the ability to prevent mistakes and failures, 2) the ability to solve problems, 3) our ability to create and maintain happiness; 4) our ability to create, select, set and achieve personal goals; 5) our professional ability, 6) the ability to face any blows of life as big and as painful as they would be; 7) the ability to create and maintain a family, a happy marriage.

68) The ability to produce positive effective ideas can increase greatly, easily and with minimum expenditure, with the help of the Internet, knowledge, positive models, which we can find using the Internet.

69) Until the creation and development of science and broadcasting them in an easy way for each, which includes the ability to create positive effective ideas,

necessary to us, respectively the creation of science, the creativity of each of us, it is necessary to look in the edited books, in the media and on the Internet, whenever existing knowledge is needed.

70) Today's knowledge can help us greatly to achieve a much happier life. Unfortunately most of this knowledge is neglected.

71) It is necessary to promote knowledge that can make us happier, can help us to achieve much easier, faster, more efficient personal goals.

72) The Internet can help us in the fastest way, most effectively, the more we find that existing knowledge can help us most to achieve personal goals.

73) Member institutions, individuals, international organizations, nonprofit organizations, private firms, etc... are necessary to carry out projects that lead to

the positive use of knowledge of as many citizens of the world to achieve personal goals, whereas today it is basically used by very few people as compared to the world's population and very little knowledge of the existent one is used.

74) Lack of insufficient jobs in some countries is primarily attributable to insufficient concern for sufficient job creation of those who have that obligation by law.

75) The so-called absence of jobs in many countries is a problem created due primarily to the lack of responsibility of state institutions and persons working to resolve these issues in each country.

About the author and his ideas

Hmm ... I do not know where to begin. It is difficult to really know someone. Often, the person on whom you stopped is difficult to decipher.

That is not the case of Gheorghe Cornel Ardelean. From the first moment I knew and he got my attention.

I recognized him immediately from the descriptions made by his colleagues: "One small, with white haired man with many books and newspapers in his hand, they said. My curiosity pushed me to address him, cheerful, open; he began to talk to me as if we knew each other for years. A person opened both to dialogue as well as current jokes. I got to know him even better when we met at Club Central. A nice company as long as you succeed not to be attracted in that part of the discussion where his future plans are. Plans that are repeated endlessly become a burden for the people around him. Not because it would be something wrong in what he says but through their very repeatability.

On several occasions I have read some of his meditations, others have been published in the magazine "Freedom in Thought".

By their simplicity and the fact that they expresses absolute truths, for those who do not take seriously the writings of Cornel Gheorghe Ardelean they may seem indeed to read seriously what to write, I bet they will find among the apparently simple lines, a message equal to a person who has suffered enormously because of human and system injustices.

The cry of a man eager for more, eager for simplicity, for the truth and for a Utopia, wishful of a perfect world.

If even 10% of what he writes would be put into practice by us, then certainly we would set ourselves and with others at the same time. Surprisingly, nobody sees that Cornel Gheorghe Ardelean even puts into practice what he writes, which means that he really believes it.

With an analytical style impossible to confuse, Mr. Cornel Gheorghe Ardelean is successful in a few lines and penetrates into the essence of truth. By this thinking, he is venturing into an area still unexplored in specialized literature.

Specialized topics are part of the absolute truths that each of us have deep within our being, so acknowledged, so obvious, so natural that no one has ventured to put them on paper.

But surely there will be many who, after reading and rereading these absolute truths will solve many of the problems of their existence. The novelty that makes Cornel Gheorghe Ardelean stand out besides putting on paper a well-known truth, is that it also leads to problem solving. It is a promising start in an area of astute competition and often an unscrupulous one.

I wish you success Mr. Ardelean and may these meditations help as many people as possible. Do not give up, continue on the path that you have chosen and maybe in the nearer or further future the world will be at least 5% as you want it to be.

Do not give up ... We ... only a few, I must admit, we are beside you.

SIMION SEBASTIAN EDUARD

Graduate of the Academy of Theater
and Film
Former journalist of the national
newspapers and Romania Libera,
Evenimentul Zilei, was Her Majesty's
Paul of Romania's adviser
a businessman resident in Italy

I invite you to visit the site: www.bigagc.com

I invite you to join my group on Facbook: (România) GrupPublic

https://www.facebook.com/groups/2283373 91695744/

We invite you to join my Facebook group: (English) GrupPublic

https://www.facebook.com/groups/BIGAGC/

I invite you to join my group on Linkedin:

https://www.linkedin.com/groups/13850051/

I invite you to contact me on Linkedin at

Ardelean Gheorghe Cornel: linkedin.com/in/gheorghe-cornel-3771971a3

I invite you to write to me by e-mail: aradforex@gmail.com

Ardelean Gheorghe Cornel
(BIGAGC)

born **03**.11.1954, in Macea, Arad County,
Email:
aradforex@gmail.com
http://www.bigagc.com/en/books

I have known the economist Cornel Ardelean for dozens of years, as a guy that outraged the thought of some who did not believe in his ideas, innovative, simply put but with a long and efficient duration. After the Revolution he proved that he is indeed a good economist by founding the first small enterprise of Arad County, in the year 1990 of the post-communist age.

I have always been by Cornel Ardelean's side, never ceasing to believe that the man can rise above his time if he wishes to and if he has the potential to do it.

SABIN BODEA
President of the Writers' League of Romania
Arad Branch

ISBN 978-973-88998-0-3
ISBN 978-973-88998-1-0

www.ingramcontent.com/pod-product-compliance
Lightning Source LLC
Chambersburg PA
CBHW050618160726

48003CB00003B/1240